THAT BLESSING WAS YOU:

a Story About Family Changes and Adoption

BY W. JAMES SMALLWOOD, JR.

ILLUSTRATED BY AYTAN KAHLAF

Published by WJS Publishing.
Illustration by Aytan Khalaf

ISBN 979-8-9912225-0-1
ISBN 979-8-9912225-1-8
ISBN 979-8-9912225-2-5

DEDICATED TO:
ROSA, BRITTNY, L.J. MATTHEW,
SALVADOR AND LILIANA.

ONE DAY, GOD BLESSED YOUR PARENTS WITH SOMETHING BRAND NEW,
SOMETHING SO PRECIOUS, AND THAT BLESSING WAS YOU!

ON THE DAY YOU WERE BORN, WE ALL FELT SUCH DELIGHT.
OUR FAMILY CELEBRATED UNTIL IT WAS NIGHT.

AS DAYS TURNED TO WEEKS, YOU CONTINUED TO GROW.
EACH ONE OF YOUR SMILES MADE OUR HEARTS OVERFLOW.

TAKING YOU SHOPPING WASN'T ALWAYS A TREAT.
SOMETIMES YOU'D LOSE TOYS, OR THE SHOES FROM YOUR FEET.

CHANGING DIAPERS WAS STINKY, THE MESSES WEREN'T FUN,
BUT MOMMY DID HER BEST BECAUSE SHE LOVED HER LITTLE ONE.

YOUR MOMMY PUSHED YOU ON THE SWINGS, EXCITEMENT IN THE AIR.
YOU BRAVELY SWUNG UP AND DOWN, WIND BLOWING THROUGH YOUR HAIR.

YOU WENT ON ADVENTURES, SPENT TIME IN THE PARK,
YOU CRAWLED AND YOU PLAYED, EVEN HID IN A CART.

YOU AND YOUR MOMMY KNEW HOW TO HAVE FUN,
AND YOU DIDN'T STOP PLAYING 'TIL SHE SAID, "WE'RE DONE!"

DADDY'S PIGGYBACK RIDES GAVE YOU NOTHING TO FEAR.
YOU'D SMILE SO BIG FROM EAR TO EAR.

BUT WHEN YOU WERE LITTLE, THINGS STARTED TO CHANGE.
MOM AND DAD WEREN'T AS FUN, THEY BEGAN ACTING STRANGE.

SOMETIMES MOMMIES AND DADDIES CAN SAY MEAN THINGS AND FIGHT,
BUT THEIR LOVE FOR YOU IS NEVER-ENDING AND WILL ALWAYS SHINE BRIGHT.

YOU SAW THEM NOW AND THEN, BUT WE WERE ALWAYS THERE,
PLAYING GAMES AND SINGING SONGS TO SHOW HOW MUCH WE CARED.

EVEN MOMMIES AND DADDIES CAN MAKE BIG MISTAKES,
AND YOUR MOMMY AND DADDY HAD TO TAKE A LONG BREAK.

IT IS NOT YOUR FAULT THAT THEY MOVED FAR APART.
EVEN MILES AWAY, THEY KEEP YOU IN THEIR HEARTS.

YOU SEE, MOMMIES AND DADDIES AREN'T PERFECT, IT'S TRUE.
WE ALL MAKE MISTAKES, AND THAT INCLUDES ME AND YOU.

IN FRONT OF THE JUDGE, WE MADE A VOW
TO LOVE AND TAKE CARE OF YOU, THEN AND NOW.

IF YOU FEEL SAD OR SCARED, IT IS OKAY.
JUST KNOW THAT AHEAD ARE MUCH HAPPIER DAYS.

CHANGE COULD MEAN A NEW HOME, AND A NEW MOMMY AND DADDY TOO.
IT COULD ALSO MEAN NEW BROTHERS AND SISTERS, AND WHERE YOU CAN BE THE BEST YOU.

ONE DAY, GOD BLESSED OUR FAMILY WITH SOMETHING NEW,
SOMETHING SO PRECIOUS AND BEAUTIFUL, AND THAT BLESSING WAS YOU.